How to Date a Feminist

a romantic comedy

by Samantha Ellis

How to Date a Feminist was first performed at the Arcola Theatre, London, on 6 September 2016

How to Date a Feminist

CAST

Tom Berish plays	Steve, a baker Ross, a newspaper editor Joe, a businessman from Israel
Sarah Daykin plays	Kate, a journalist Carina, a stone-carver Morag, an activist

Director	**Matthew Lloyd**
Designer	**Carla Goodman**
Lighting Designer	**Joe Price**
Sound Design	**John Leonard** **Philip Matejtschuk**
Assistant Director	**Selena Lu**
Stage Manager	**Samantha Gardiner**
Technical Manager	**Sari Shrayteh**
Press Representation	**Liz Hyder**
PR Liaison	**Lewis Frost**

THE COMPANY

TOM BERISH

Tom read English at Cambridge and trained at LAMDA. His theatre credits include *Paper Dolls* (Tricycle); *The Taming of the Shrew* (RSC); *Family Business, Perfect Match* (Watford Palace); *The School for Scandal* (Park); *The Sting, Are We Nearly There Yet?* (Wilton's Music Hall); *Listen, We're Family* (Wilton's/JW3); *Of Mice and Men* (Watermill); *Romeo and Juliet* (Royal Lyceum). His television credits include *The Village, The Last Heroes of D-Day* and *Doctors* for the BBC.

SARAH DAYKIN

Sarah Daykin is best known for being one half of sister comedy duo 'Toby' who have had several successful runs at the Edinburgh Fringe and Soho Theatre. Her extensive television credits include *Josh, Fleabag, Together, Cockroaches, Dead Boss, Anna and Katy, Live at the Electric* and *Chickens.*

SAMANTHA ELLIS – Writer

Theatre credits include *Operation Magic Carpet* (Polka); *Cling To Me Like Ivy* (Birmingham Repertory Theatre/tour; also published by Nick Hern Books); *Starlore For Beginners and Other Plays, Patching Havoc* (Theatre503); *This Time I Win* (Agent 160/Cardiff Millennium Centre); *The Thousand and Second Night* (LAMDA); *A Sudden Visitation of Calamity* (Menagerie); *Startle Response* (Young Vic Workshop); *Martin's Wedding* (Blind Summit/BAC); *Use Me As Your Cardigan* (Jackson's Lane); *Feel the Plastic* (Camden People's Theatre); *The Candy Jar* (Edinburgh Fringe; runner-up in NSDF's International Student Drama Competition).

Radio includes: *Sugar and Snow* (BBC Radio 4/Hampstead).

Samantha is also the author of the non-fiction book *How to Be a Heroine* (Chatto & Windus).

SAMANTHA GARDINER – Stage Manager

Upon graduating from the Western Australian Academy of Performing Arts Samantha moved to London to further her stage-management career. Samantha's UK stage management credits include *Sparks* at The Old Red Lion Theatre; *Cosi* at The King's Head Theatre; *Knife Edge* with The Big House including its encore run for Open Court at the Royal Court. She was also the assistant stage manager on Grange Park Opera's *Samson et Dalila* and Opera Holland Park's *La Cenerentola*.

CARLA GOODMAN – Designer

Carla trained as a set and costume designer in Nottingham, London and New York.

Design credits include *Rise* (Old Vic Outdoors); *Exposure, Pig Farm* (St James); *NotMoses* (Arts); *Romeo and Juliet* (Orange Tree); *Miss Julie* (Et Cetera); *Heartbreak Hotel* (The Jetty, Greenwich); *Truce* (New Wimbledon); *What Flows Past the Baltic* (Nottingham Playhouse); *Theatre Uncut* (Southwark Playhouse/Traverse/Soho); *Listen, We're Family* (Wilton's Music Hall); *Ariodante* (Royal Academy of Music); *Mush and Me* (Bush); *I Am Your Neighbour, Skeen, King Lear* (Ovalhouse); *A New Face for Fast Times* (Soho); *The Love Project* (Arts Depot/UK tour); *Nola* (Underbelly Edinburgh); *Step Live!* (Royal Academy of Dance/Southbank Centre); *Kitchen to Measure* (Arcola); *Mr Happiness* (The Old Vic Tunnels); *Bud Take the Wheel* (Shaw/Underbelly Edinburgh).

JOHN LEONARD – Co-Sound Designer

John started work in theatre sound over forty years ago and during that time he has provided soundtracks for theatres all over the world, written an acclaimed guide to theatre sound, won various awards and published several collections of sound effects. He is a Fellow of The Guildhall School and an Honorary Fellow of The Hong Kong Academy of Performing Arts.

MATTHEW LLOYD – Director

Matthew is a freelance theatre director and producer. Previous credits include the Olivier-nominated *Duet for One* and the multi-award-winning *The Fastest Clock in the Universe*. He has commissioned and directed new play premieres for the Almeida, the Royal Court, the Royal Exchange, Hampstead, the Bush, Soho and many of the UK's leading regional playhouses. Recent work includes *The Line* (Arcola); *The Welsh Boy* and *The Good Soldier* (Ustinov Studio, Bath) and two self-created verbatim shows, *The Pilgrimage Project* and *Listen, We're Family* (Wilton's Music Hall & JW3). He was formerly Joint Artistic Director and Chief Executive of the Royal Exchange Theatre, Manchester, where his many productions included the award-winning *An Experiment with an Air-Pump, The Illusion* and *Dreaming* (West End transfer). He was also Associate Director of Hampstead Theatre, where his credits included *Slavs!, Ghost from a Perfect Place* and the Olivier Award-winning *The Lucky Ones*.

SELENA LU – Assistant Director

Selena Lu is an independent theatre director and researcher, based in London and Beijing. She has a BA in Politics, Psychology and Sociology from the University of Cambridge and is an MFA candidate in Theatre Directing at East15 Acting School.

Documentary and community-based theatre projects include *The Way to Walden* (Beijing, 2015); *Period Pain Monologues* (Cambridge, 2014; Beijing and Helsinki, 2015); *PoseTSD* (Beijing, 2016); *Knife Edge* (AD with The Big House Company, London, 2016).

PHILIP MATEJTSCHUK – Co-Sound Designer

Philip is a freelance sound designer and composer, and holds a PgDip in Sound Design for the Theatre from RADA. Recent credits include *The Burnt Part Boys* (Park); *I'm Getting my Act Together and Taking it on the Road* (Jermyn Street); *Maggie & Pierre* (Finborough); *Better Together* (Jack Studio); *A Secret Life* (Theatre503/promenade); *Spitting Image, Cosi* (King's Head). Philip has been nominated twice for the Best Sound Designer Offie Award, for *Dead Party Animals* in 2014 and earlier this year for *Sea Life*, both at The Hope Theatre. Other credits include *Orphans* (Southwark Playhouse); *Chew* (Etcetera); *The Haunting, 1938: Hitler Takes Vienna, Leonce & Lena, rockpaperscissors* (Jack Studio); *Hello Again, Baby* (Hope); *Caught* (Pleasance, Islington); *Iphigenia in Tauris* (Rose Playhouse); *Othello* (Rose Playhouse/tour inc. New York) and *Mother Courage and Her Children* (Platform Theatre, KX). Associate sound designer credits include *Pig Farm* (St. James); *Stevie* (Hampstead) and *King Lear* (Cockpit). Philip is Head of Sound at Italia Conti Academy of Theatre Arts. Contact him @philmatejtschuk.

JOE PRICE – Lighting Designer

Lighting design credits include *Some Girl(s)* (Buckland Theatre Company/Park); *Around the World in 80 Days* (Blue Apple/Theatre Royal Winchester); *Fossils* (Bucket Club/UK tour); *Daughter of the Forest* (Komola Collective/UK tour); *The Love I Feel is Red* (Tobacco Factory/ Zion Community Space); *Miss Julie* (Buckland Theatre Company/ Etcetera); *The Selfish Giant* (Blue Apple/Tower Arts Centre); *Some People Talk About Violence* (Barrel Organ/Camden People's Theatre); *Dry Land* (Damsel Productions/Jermyn Street); *The Hitchhiker's Guide to the Family* (Ideas Tap Award, Edinburgh Fringe); *A Third* (Fat Git/ Finborough); *Alternative Routes* (National Dance Company Wales, Dance House WMC); *The Duchess of Malfi* (Richard Burton Theatre Company, RWCMD); *Animal/Endless Ocean* (Royal Court/National Theatre Wales/Richard Burton Theatre Company/Gate); *Y Twr* (Invertigo/UK tour); *I Feel Fine* (Fat Git/New Diorama). Relight credits include *Kite* (Wrong Crowd/Soho/UK tour); *Blink* (nabokov/Soho/UK tour/Brits off Broadway); *Living Without Fear, Hamlet* (Blue Apple/UK tour); *Wasted* (Paines Plough/UK tour); *Some Like It Hotter* (Fresh Glory Productions/UK tour).

SARI SHRAYTEH – Technical Manager

Sari is a twenty-four-year-old theatre and film practitioner from Beirut. He got his BA in communication arts at the Lebanese American University. He has worked in numerous positions including: Stage Manager at The Act Dubai, Stage Manager at The Box in New York, Technical Director at Beirut 8:30, in addition to freelance work in light, sound and set design. He is currently getting his MFA in theatre directing at East15 in hopes of combining his acquired skills to create new social, community theatres in the Middle East.

Arcola Theatre is one of London's leading off-West End theatres.

Locally engaged and internationally minded, Arcola stages a diverse programme of plays, operas and musicals. World-class productions from major artists appear alongside cutting-edge work from the most exciting emerging companies.

Arcola delivers one of London's most extensive community engagement programmes, creating over 5000 opportunities every year. By providing research and development space to diverse artists, Arcola champions theatre that's more engaging and representative. Its pioneering environmental initiatives are internationally renowned, and aim to make Arcola the world's first carbon-neutral theatre.

GAME CHANGERS
Graham & Christine Benson
Roger Bradburn & Helen Main
Katie Bradford
Andrew Cripps
Sarah Morrison
Mike Newell
Nicholas & Lesley Pryor

TRAILBLAZERS
Vicky Eltringham
Katrin Maeurich
Jane Haynes
Catrin Evans

with thanks to all of our Supporters and Volunteers

MEHMET ERGEN
Artistic Director

LEYLA NAZLI
Executive Producer

BEN TODD
Executive Director

JOE COCHRANE
Assistant Bar Manager

NICK CONNAUGHTON
Creative Engagement Manager

FEIMATTA CONTEH
Sustainability Manager

NICK CRIPPS
IT Manager

CHARLOTTE CROFT
Front of House & Box Office Manager (Maternity Leave)

JACK GAMBLE
Communications and Marketing Manager

GEOFF HENSE
Technical Manager

RICHARD KEMP-HARPER
Business Development Manager

MIRIAM MAHONY
Front of House & Box Office Manager (Maternity Cover)

REBECCA MARTIN
Creative Engagement Coordinator

MARTIN POOT
Software Engineer

JONNY POWELL
Bar Manager

LAURA ROLINSON
Operations Manager

RICHARD SPEIR
Production Assistant

DAVID TODD
Facilities Manager

www.arcolatheatre.com
020 7503 1646

HOW TO DATE A FEMINIST

a romantic comedy

Samantha Ellis

Acknowledgements

This play began as a ten-minute short for The Miniaturists. I'm very grateful to Stephen Sharkey for letting me explore, and to Miranda Cook and David Hartley for exploring with me, and to Henry Bell, Brigid Larmour, Emily Holt, Eva-Jane Willis and Tom Berish for two very illuminating readings since. Thank you for useful thoughts and provocations along the way to Emma Ayech, Maddy Costa, Heloïse Sénéchal, Jude Cook, Jonathan Thake, Dominic Leggett and Paul King, and, as ever, to the Dog House writers, Robin Booth, Nick Harrop, Matthew Morrison and Ben Musgrave. Thank you also to my fantastic agent Nick Quinn, and to Matthew Lloyd for believing in the play and making it happen, along with Tom Berish, Sarah Daykin, and everyone at the Arcola Theatre and at Nick Hern Books.

S.E.

Characters

STEVE, *thirty, a baker*
KATE, *thirty, a journalist*
ROSS, *forty, Kate's ex-boyfriend, a newspaper editor*
CARINA, *thirty-five, Steve's ex-fiancée, a stone-carver*
JOE, *seventy-five, Kate's father, a businessman from Israel*
MORAG, *sixty, Steve's mother, an activist from Scotland*

The play was written for a cast of two, with the following doubling:

STEVE/ROSS/JOE
KATE/CARINA/MORAG

The play can also be performed by a cast of six.

This text went to press before the end of rehearsals and so may differ slightly from the play as performed.

ACT ONE

Scene One

A bare stage apart from a dressing-up box full of costumes – unless indicated, all costume changes happen on stage.

A winter night, a London alleyway. Music drifts out from a bar. STEVE *runs on, pulling* KATE *along with him. Both are in coats.*

KATE. What is it? What? I'm staying out for one minute then you have to dance with me.

STEVE. I can't dance.

KATE. Course you can.

STEVE. I get self-conscious. I can't turn my head off.

KATE. Everyone can dance!

STEVE. Kate. *Kate.*

KATE. OH! Oh my God.

STEVE *is down on one knee, holding an engagement ring.*

STEVE. Before you say anything, I want to apologise. I want to apologise for the patriarchy.

KATE. You what?

STEVE. Don't laugh.

KATE (*laughing*). Okay. Why?

STEVE. I just think if we're going to spend the rest of our lives together, we don't want all that hanging over us.

KATE. All what?

STEVE. Well okay: Ancient Greece. Women were property. Apart from the Vestal Virgins. And in Egypt, round about the same time…

KATE (*laughs*). Egypt?

STEVE. Just let me – bride-burning. Female genital mutilation. Domestic violence. Chattel marriage. Unequal pay. Footbinding.

KATE. Steve!

STEVE. It went on a thousand years.

KATE. I know but –

STEVE. They broke the arches of women's feet.

KATE. I'm not Chinese.

STEVE. They turned them into little points. Like sharpened pencils. Have you seen those pictures? X-rays. I mean, the *pain*.

KATE. My feet are fine.

STEVE. Look, you're a woman, I'm a man –

KATE. I hate when you take everything back to first principles. I know I'm a woman.

STEVE. Okay so marriage is problematic. Even if we write our own vows, it still means signing up to… a lot. I think we should mark it. And I know you've had some bad experiences, like with your dad.

KATE. My dad?

STEVE. When I think about the patriarchy, I think about your dad.

KATE. My dad's had a really tough life!

STEVE. I know.

KATE. He grew up in a refugee camp. He didn't have time to get politically correct.

STEVE. I just want us to start fresh.

KATE. Fresh?

STEVE. I love you, I think! (*Beat.*) I want us to go on a journey! Into the future, into chaos and uncertainty and – we could be together sixty years! With funny-faced babies and a tumbledown house and moth-eaten jumpers and stupid jokes and scraps of poems and candlelit baths. Or we could be scrabbling for potatoes in the ruins of our civilisation. You know? We just don't know. And if we're going to navigate our way through all *that*, don't you think we should try to go forward without any shame or bitterness or regret?

KATE. No. No I don't. Why won't you just propose? For fuck's sake. Propose!

STEVE. I just did.

Scene Two

No blackout, no scene change. The music stops, and lights change to a summer garden. It's a fancy-dress party, eighteen months earlier. They take off their coats. He's dressed as Robin Hood – with laddered tights. She's dressed as Wonder Woman.

KATE. Are those ladders in your tights or stairways to heaven? I never thought I'd get to use that line on a man.

STEVE. They're just really cheap tights. I got them at a service station.

KATE. That is not where you buy tights.

STEVE. I'll bear that in mind.

KATE. Can you do me a favour? See Superman over there?

STEVE. The one with Jenny?

KATE. He's not *with* her. What's she come as, anyway?

STEVE. 'Medieval tavern wench', she says.

KATE. If she'd dressed like that in medieval times, they'd have hanged her for a witch.

STEVE. That's just Jenny being Jenny.

KATE. Does it *look* like he's with her? Superman?

STEVE. Well he has got his hand up her skirt.

KATE. We broke up on Wednesday. Him and me.

STEVE. Oh. Sorry.

KATE. It's fine, honestly. I'm over it. But: could you just, I'm not saying *flirt*, but maybe look a bit… *dazzled*?

STEVE. Dazzled?

KATE. I'm not a total dog.

STEVE. Of course not but –

KATE. I'm dressed as Wonder Woman; the least you could do is look at my pants. That's the whole point of Wonder Woman; you can see her pants.

STEVE. That isn't the whole point of –

KATE. He wanted me to come as Lois Lane. And I love Lois Lane. She's one of the reasons I became a journalist. And they *are* the perfect couple. But under the circumstances, as of Wednesday, I didn't want to match his costume.

STEVE. Superman and Lois Lane are a *terrible* couple.

KATE. What? Why?

STEVE. He can't be *super* when he's *with* her!

KATE. Yes but –

STEVE. And if she's such a good journalist how come it takes her so long to work out who he is? Just because he's wearing glasses! And when she does work it out, he erases her memory.

KATE. Yes but by kissing her.

STEVE. That doesn't make it any less controlling.

KATE. You're funny.

STEVE. Wonder Woman's much better. She can bounce bullets off her bracelets, burst a dinghy with her tiara, deflect a meteorite, survive without oxygen in outer space. She's a fantastic role model for girls. *And* she's in a proper relationship.

KATE. What, with *Steve Trevor*?

STEVE (*delighted*). You know Wonder Woman's boyfriend's name! I've never met anyone who knew his name. Apart from my mum.

KATE. He's pathetic.

STEVE. He's a *fighter pilot*.

KATE. But he always has to get rescued. And he can't fly her plane because it's invisible. He can't see the controls. Poor Steve Trevor. With his custard-coloured hair. I always felt sorry for him.

STEVE. I was named after him.

KATE. You weren't.

STEVE. My mum just really loved Wonder Woman.

KATE. Me too. She's cool, when she spins round and her clothes spin off –

STEVE. My mum was more into her as a symbol of female power. So. (*Puts out a hand.*) Steve.

KATE (*shaking hands*). Kate. She didn't bother with the Trevor part?

STEVE. That might have been overkill.

KATE. Hey, so why Robin Hood?

STEVE. He's a brilliant ethical hero. Stealing from the rich to give to the poor. He basically invented the welfare state. *And* the green movement. He's way ahead of his time.

KATE. But isn't he always kidnapping Maid Marian and carrying her off on his horse?

STEVE. Not in the original. If you look at the fifteenth-century ballads, Maid Marian's a heroine in her own right.

KATE. You read fifteenth-century ballads to get ready for a fancy-dress party?

STEVE. I like to be prepared.

KATE. Clearly.

STEVE. And in the ballads, they're totally equal. She's always cross-dressing and winning swordfights. She's as tough as any of the Merry Men.

KATE (*looking over at Superman*). Why's he flirting with Jenny? She's not even pretty. And he says all women over thirty look raddled. Do I look raddled?

STEVE. You're beautiful.

KATE. I'm not.

STEVE. No, honestly, you're very pretty.

KATE. I wasn't fishing. Don't go overboard.

STEVE. Why did you break up?

KATE. I caught him shagging this intern. My intern actually. He's my editor. And he got me this intern like it was a favour. Like she'd be helping me. Then I find them in the newsroom loos. The *ladies'*. I'm standing there with my tampon in my hand and they're coming out the cubicle all flushed and dreamy-eyed. And he isn't even sorry. He says he wants an open relationship.

STEVE. It sounds like you've had a lucky escape.

KATE. He's very clever. He's an excellent editor. He's unflinching, the way he looks at the world. (*Beat.*) But he is *bad*.

STEVE. So why do you like him?

KATE. I like bad men.

STEVE. What do you mean?

KATE. I always go out with cads and bounders. If you lined up all my exes… (*Counting them off on her fingers.*) There was the alcoholic. He made extravagant declarations of love but never remembered them in the morning. The Marxist liked having sex on the bus; he thought beds were bourgeois. Never sit on the back seat of a London bus. The musician was feckless, but he had so much soul. When we broke up, he was so heartbroken, he smashed up his violin.

STEVE. These men really do sound bad.

KATE. Oh and the puppeteer… he turned out to be manipulative.

STEVE. Of course.

KATE. And Superman. I mean, Ross. That's his name.

STEVE. We know why he's bad.

KATE. I'm giving you too much information.

STEVE. You're giving me redundant information. Why don't you stop liking bad men?

KATE. You can't help what you like.

STEVE. Of course you can. You've got a brain, you can decide things.

KATE. It's not a brain thing, it's a heart thing. And anyway, I can't change. People don't change.

STEVE. Of course we do!

KATE. You're very certain.

STEVE. I couldn't get up in the morning if I didn't believe people changed. I grew up at Greenham Common.

KATE. At the peace camp?

STEVE. I was only little. I mostly just collected firewood and played my kazoo.

KATE. Wow.

STEVE. If we could stop nuclear war at Greenham, you can stop fancying bad men.

KATE. Did you stop nuclear war at Greenham Common?

STEVE. Has there been a nuclear war?

KATE. The thing is: I've got to go out with bad men because I'm really terrible at flirting! I throw up barriers, I *talk*. I need someone confident to blast through all that. I need someone to pounce. And nice men don't pounce.

Music shifts. It is later that evening. KATE *is with Superman aka* ROSS, *her ex. He is played by the actor playing* STEVE.

ROSS. What happened to Lois Lane?

KATE. I decided I didn't want to match your costume. Not after Wednesday. You're not Superman. You can't erase my memory with a kiss. Not that I want you to kiss me.

ROSS. Pity. I was looking forward to your Lois Lane. Slinky pencil skirt. Blouse slashed to here. Proper heels.

KATE. I came as my own superheroine, thank you.

ROSS (*looks her up and down*). So I see.

KATE. Don't do that.

ROSS. Do what?

KATE. Look me up and down. Like you can see through my clothes. Like you're going to rip them off me later.

ROSS. You never know your luck.

KATE. We're not doing this.

ROSS. It's not a quiet costume. It attracts comment.

KATE. You've forfeited your right to comment.

ROSS. You're usually so demure. You dress like a Nice Jewish Girl. You dress neurotic. It's nice to see you let go.

KATE. I'm not up for an open relationship. Stop asking.

ROSS. Your loss.

KATE. We're not even going to be friends. Just colleagues.

ROSS. I'm your boss, if you want to play it that way. You're my employee.

KATE. Yes. Good. Not even colleagues. I feel lots better.

ROSS. Did you have a nice chat with Steve?

KATE. How do you know his name?

ROSS. He used to be engaged to Jenny's sister, Carina. I don't know why he's still hanging around.

KATE. Carina? The *welder*?

ROSS. She's actually a stone-carver. But never let the truth get in the way of a good story.

KATE. What happened?

ROSS. She broke his heart. So he's definitely in the market for a mercy fuck. That really would be heroic. Superheroic.

KATE. Go away. Just leave me alone.

Music changes. It is later in the evening. STEVE *is talking to his ex,* CARINA, *who has made a gesture towards fancy dress by wearing a cat-ears headband. She is played by the actor playing* KATE.

STEVE. No, it's good. Minimalist. I like it.

CARINA. I hate fancy dress.

STEVE. Unlike your sister.

CARINA. She likes it too much.

STEVE. It's amazing you came out of the same womb.

CARINA. I can nearly *see* her womb in that outfit.

STEVE. It's not that bad.

CARINA. It is. Why didn't she just come as a prostitute and be done with it?

STEVE (*laughs*). Don't be mean.

CARINA. You're right. Your mum would call me out for slut-shaming. And she'd be right.

STEVE. How is my mum?

CARINA (*laughs*). Don't ask me!

STEVE. You see her more than I do.

CARINA. How are you, Steve?

STEVE. All right, Carina. How are you? How's work?

CARINA. Good. Great. I'm making gargoyles for this church in Suffolk. Dragons, monsters, fantastical beasts.

STEVE. Scaring off those demons, warding off that evil.

CARINA. Gargoyles don't do that. They divert water from the walls. Their mouths are spouts. They're rain gutters. I've only told you this about a thousand times.

STEVE. I shouldn't have come.

CARINA. No, I'm glad you did. I told Jenny to invite you. I thought, it's crazy, I see your mum all the time; why not see you? It's more normal, isn't it? We can be friends.

STEVE. Yes. Friends.

CARINA. I'd better help Jenny with the drinks. She's doing dark and stormies and she always puts in too much lime.

STEVE. Do you want a hand?

CARINA. No.

STEVE. Okay.

The music changes. It's later in the evening. STEVE *and* KATE *are talking again.* KATE *has hiccups.*

KATE. I *hate* hiccups.

STEVE. Here. (*Pours some water out of a jug.*) Drink from the wrong side.

KATE. What?

STEVE. You know, drink backwards. (*Pours another glass.*) I'll do it with you.

KATE. Do what?

STEVE. Tip forwards. And just drink the whole lot, without stopping.

They do. When they've finished, they're laughing, and her hiccups are gone.

KATE. That wasn't water!

STEVE. Who puts vodka in a jug?

KATE. *Jenny.*

STEVE. We just downed that.

KATE. *Backwards!*

STEVE. You're a natural.

KATE. And I'm healed!

STEVE. Shall we get out of here?

KATE. Yes! Take me to Sherwood Forest! Carry me off on your horse!

STEVE. We could go to the pub on the corner.

KATE. Fuck that. There's that chip shop. You know. With the big fish in the window. The massive fish. The smiling fish. You know.

STEVE. I don't think I know the massive, smiling fish.

KATE. Oh you must. You've got to see it. Oh My Cod!

STEVE. Are you okay?

KATE. It's the name of the shop. Oh My Cod. That's the other thing that's great about it. Don't you love puns? I love puns. (*Has got out her phone and is looking at the map in confusion.*) I know it's here somewhere. It's really near. You do want chips, right?

STEVE. More than anything.

KATE (*at the phone*). Come on. Come on.

STEVE. Maybe turn it round?

KATE. I can't read maps. I'm such a girl.

STEVE. Don't say that. Now I can't help you.

KATE. Why?

STEVE. I'll feel like a chauvinist.

KATE. Come on. We can be stuck at this party. Or we could be eating the greatest chips in London. Just make it work.

He wavers.

You literally can't do it. Wow. Come on. Abandon your principles! For me.

STEVE. I'll *show* you. I'm not doing it for you.

KATE. No, fine, empower me. But hurry up.

STEVE. You don't turn the phone, you turn the map. See, it's got a compass. Here.

KATE. This way?

STEVE. *This* way. You see, there's a little blue arrow, it shows which way you're facing and then you just –

KATE. Let's go!

They set off.

Scene Three

STEVE *and* KATE, *at a chip shop. Tinny music plays.*

STEVE. What is it you like about bad men?

KATE. I don't know… I like men who are tall and dark and smouldering.

STEVE. You mean you like brown hair.

KATE. I like *chivalry.*

STEVE. I like chivalry. But why can't it go both ways? Why can't women be chivalrous to men? Why do I always have to be the *outside* of the spoon?

KATE. Heathcliff. I like Heathcliff.

STEVE. Heathcliff hangs puppies.

KATE. His son hangs puppies. Heathcliff hangs a dog.

STEVE. You say it like it's better.

KATE. I don't like him *because* he hangs a dog. I just like him.

STEVE. Either way, your dog's getting killed.

KATE. I don't actually have a dog.

STEVE. Do you want to save these men from themselves? Is that the attraction?

KATE. No.

STEVE. Do you want to tame them?

KATE. No.

STEVE. You want to *change* them. You think the more they change for you, the more it proves they love you.

KATE. No. If they changed they wouldn't be bad any more, and I wouldn't fancy them.

STEVE. I suppose that's logical.

KATE. Course it is.

STEVE. You do know romantic fiction is the female equivalent of men watching porn?

KATE. Are we comparing Emily Brontë's *Wuthering Heights* to porn?

STEVE. It creates unrealistic expectations.

KATE. Wanting Heathcliff is not like wanting women to have no body hair.

STEVE. Its effects are the same. Women get waxed, men take up boxing.

KATE. You think you're a better feminist than me.

STEVE. I know I am.

KATE. I'm the only woman on the newsdesk. Every day I'm writing about the way austerity disproportionately affects women, I'm covering stories on abuse, and equal pay. I follow Everyday Sexism on Twitter. I think Caitlin Moran has done a lot for women with cystitis. But you can't control what's in your heart and in my heart, I like lipstick. Cupcakes. Heathcliff.

STEVE. You don't.

KATE. I do.

STEVE. No, you just think you do. Because the world is very messed up.

KATE. Well how do I tell the difference between the things I want but only think I want, and the things I want but shouldn't want and the things I want that I *can* want?

STEVE. It seems pretty obvious to me. But then I don't want lipstick, cupcakes, Heathcliff.

KATE. What's wrong with cupcakes?

STEVE. They're not real cakes.

KATE. Oh you like *man's* cakes. Big, strong cakes.

STEVE. I like a proper ratio of cake to icing.

KATE. You like more cake than icing.

STEVE. I don't like decapitating a cake, I don't like injecting icing into the body of a cake.

KATE. You make it sound immoral!

STEVE. A cupcake is an inherently selfish cake; you can't share it.

KATE. Oh. I love that.

STEVE. Don't make fun of me.

KATE. No, really. You've destroyed my love of cupcakes.

STEVE. Excellent.

KATE. I still want Heathcliff though.

STEVE. Baby steps.

KATE. You are so patronising.

STEVE. It was a joke!

KATE. Can you drive?

STEVE. No.

KATE. Carve?

STEVE. I'm a vegetarian.

KATE. Can you iron?

STEVE. Why?

KATE. Because I burn shirts. I'm to shirts what the Sheriff of Nottingham was to peasants. And because all men should drive, carve and iron.

STEVE. You can't be this reactionary.

KATE (*shrugs*). Sorry.

STEVE. Tell me about your dad.

KATE. My dad's nothing to do with it! I have had time to think for myself.

STEVE. But he's not a feminist.

KATE. He's… old-fashioned. He likes it when I wear a dress. He opens doors. But he's not oppressing anyone.

STEVE. Is he oppressing your mum?

KATE. They're divorced.

STEVE. Oh, sorry.

KATE. My mum taught me all this stuff, like: blue and green must never be seen, or blue and black, or brown and grey. And to blot lipstick three times, and jump into my perfume, and never bake when you've got your period or the cake won't rise. And then she read Germaine Greer and she left.

STEVE. Really?

KATE. Yep. *The Female Eunuch*. It was my copy! She found it in my schoolbag, stayed up all night reading it and in the morning she got herself a lawyer. My dad thought she'd gone mad. It came out of nowhere. He thought they were happy. He thought they'd be married forever. And I'd marry an accountant and live in Hendon and have them over every Friday night.

STEVE. You could still marry an accountant and live in Hendon.

KATE. All the accountants are married. They married the girls they used to hang out with at the bagel shop. I was going into Camden; they were changing the words of 'Yellow Submarine' to 'We all live in a house in Golders Green'. Now they've all got ten-year-olds. I was just so desperate not to end up in the kitchen like my mum. I never learned to cook.

STEVE. You are a feminist.

KATE. I totally shot myself in the foot. I live on picnic food. I can't remember the last time I had a hot dinner. I'd be a better feminist if I could fend for myself.

STEVE. Come to my bakery some time. I'll cook you dinner.

KATE. You're a baker? How come?

STEVE. I wanted to work for myself. I was on and off protest sites growing up so I only got one A level, I couldn't go to university. And I love working with live yeast. That sounded wrong.

KATE. Hence the cakes.

STEVE. Hence the cakes. Why journalism?

KATE. I wanted a job that was about finding things out and telling people about them. Being curious. I didn't realise it would be so cynical or I'd be fighting over semicolons, and everyone would be trying to push me onto the lifestyle pages because that's what women write. Lois Lane never had to put up with that shit. Are you where you thought you'd be?

STEVE. At Greenham, my mum made me this placard. It read 'When I Grow Up I Want To Be Alive.' And I am.

KATE. You had low expectations.

STEVE. I don't listen to Bob Dylan any more. Too many late nights round campfires with people playing him on out-of-tune guitars. I don't eat as many lentils as I used to. But I'm still a feminist. Are you where you thought you'd be?

KATE. I thought I'd have this great love. It would be love, real love, and he'd deflect my life. He'd take me in a new direction. And it would be wild and passionate and – what?

STEVE. No, go on.

KATE. What is it?

STEVE. You've got ketchup on your face.

KATE. Oh.

She wipes her face.

STEVE. Define 'real love'.

KATE. Love, real love! When you hold out your heart and say: do what you want with it! Crush it! Stamp on it! Destroy me! Make me new.

STEVE. My idea of love's more gentle.

KATE. Gentle? How did that work out with Jenny's scary sister?

STEVE. Carina's not scary.

KATE. She is famously terrifying.

STEVE. She's a strong woman.

KATE. Are you still in love with her?

STEVE. We're friends. Or trying to be. We've still got loads of friends in common. She and my mum share an allotment.

KATE. What?

STEVE. You don't give up an allotment in London.

KATE. But it's so disloyal.

STEVE. They bring courgettes round when they get a glut. And rhubarb.

KATE. Hang on. (*Puts her Wonder Woman lasso around* STEVE.) Now you are wearing the lasso of truth.

STEVE. It's pretty flimsy. For a lasso.

KATE. I made it myself. It didn't come as part of the costume. But: you can't lie now.

STEVE. I can't?

KATE. Nope. You have to tell the truth. Come on, I told you about my exes. Why did you break up?

STEVE. She said she didn't love me, just the idea of me. I'm still paying off the engagement ring. My credit-card bill comes through every month like a knife in the heart.

KATE. She didn't give you back the ring?

STEVE. I didn't ask for it.

KATE. Did anyone ever tell you you're too nice?

STEVE. I *was* going to offer you my last chip.

He eats the chip.

KATE. It was cold, wasn't it?

STEVE. It wasn't at its peak.

The music cuts out.

KATE. We should go.

STEVE. We should.

Reluctantly, they stand up. She has an idea, and starts rummaging in her bag.

KATE. Let me fix those ladders.

STEVE. What?

KATE. Your tights. Clear nail varnish. It stops them running. Let me.

STEVE. What? Oh. Okay.

She fixes the ladders in his tights. It's intimate.

KATE. There. You're fixed.

Scene Four

Lights change. Both change into whatever they were wearing the first night at his place, a week later.

STEVE. May I kiss you?

KATE. Course.

He kisses her.

STEVE. May I kiss you again, with my tongue?

KATE. Yes…

He kisses her.

STEVE. May I kiss your collarbone?

KATE (*laughs*). Um, *yeah*.

He kisses her collarbone.

STEVE. May I kiss your shoulder?

KATE. Steve…

STEVE. I'm sorry, am I going too fast?

KATE. No!

STEVE. I'm sorry…

KATE. Don't stop.

STEVE. But…

KATE. Can't you just…

STEVE. If you don't want me to kiss your shoulder…

KATE. This 'may I' business…

STEVE. Is it a bit formal?

KATE. You're talking like you're on the sex offenders' register!

STEVE. I was hoping you'd be up for explicit verbal consent.

KATE. For what?

STEVE. I need this to be transparent and honest. I don't want to have to be tough and unemotional and insensitive and *brooding* and unavailable and strong and silent.

KATE. You could maybe be a bit more silent.

STEVE. I just want to make sure I'm doing what you want.

KATE. I want you to do what *you* want.

STEVE. But that's just like saying you want to be ravished.

KATE. Well maybe something on the ravishing spectrum.

STEVE. What would you normally do now? With one of your bad men.

KATE. I'd go into the bathroom and then I'd emerge.

STEVE. Do you mean you need the loo?

KATE. No!

STEVE. What then?

KATE. I can't *tell* you. That's the point.

STEVE. Well how can I…?

KATE. Okay, fine. I fix my mascara, whip out my chicken fillets, stick in some KY jelly –

STEVE. Wait, sorry, *chicken fillets*?

KATE. Those silicone things.

STEVE. You *emerge* with smaller breasts?

KATE (*proudly*). A whole cup size.

STEVE. Hang on: KY jelly?

KATE. I get nervous. And it's hard to look like I'm excited. And men get offended. It's just nerves, so…

STEVE. I'm getting nervous now.

KATE. No, don't…

STEVE. You said you only fancy bad men. And I'm not a bad man.

KATE. But I want to change.

STEVE. Yes but not by faking excitement. I feel awful.

KATE. Okay, look: I'll prove how much I want to be here. How long did it take you to get ready for tonight? You had a shower, changed your shirt; that's, what, twenty minutes?

STEVE. I didn't have a shower. Sorry.

KATE. I took eight hours. I took the day off. That's how much I want you.

STEVE. What did you do for eight hours?

KATE. Manicure, pedicure, Epsom salts bath, fake tan, fake eyelashes, eyebrow thread, bikini wax, coloured contact lenses, kissproof lipstick – that's to make it stay on, by the way, not to stop you kissing me.

STEVE. Those aren't your real eyes?

KATE. They're the same colour as my eyes, just a little more intense; like I dye my hair its own colour, just a little more intense. Don't you like it?

STEVE. It's just, to me, you looked really pretty in that chip shop with ketchup on your face. I hate that you think you have to trick me.

KATE. I just want to look my best.

STEVE. Why not just look like you?

KATE. This is what women do. We move around in a cloud of smoke and perfume and lure you in. We're mysterious.

STEVE. You don't have to be mysterious. And you could just tell me what you want.

KATE. I can't.

STEVE. You can.

KATE. I feel shy.

STEVE. Don't feel shy!

KATE. I do…

STEVE. You were so confident before.

KATE. Before.

STEVE. Say anything – there's no judgement. I'm unshockable.

KATE. It's not that.

STEVE. What is it?

KATE (*in tears*). I don't know what I want.

STEVE. What's wrong?

KATE. I'm not some liberated sex goddess.

STEVE. Okay.

KATE. No one's ever asked me what I want. And I don't know! I should know. But I don't.

STEVE. That's okay…

KATE. It's not okay! I'm scared. I shouldn't be scared. But I am.

STEVE. You can be scared.

KATE. I feel really stupid. You don't want me crying and not knowing what I want and, fuck, I'm sorry. I'm really sorry.

STEVE. Can I hold you?

KATE. I'll get mascara on your shirt. I've got three layers on. (*Crying.*) It's inky black. It's the worst for stains. And I like that shirt.

STEVE. I'm just going to hold you, okay?

He holds her.

KATE. I'm sorry.

STEVE. It's not a sorry thing.

KATE. I feel like I've got no skin.

STEVE. It's frightening being honest.

KATE. Yes.

STEVE. Not bad-frightening, though?

KATE. No. Not bad-frightening.

STEVE. Will you… will you stay here a minute? I'll come back. Just a minute.

KATE. Where are you going? Steve?

He's already gone. When he returns, he's got a loaf of bread.

Bread. You brought me bread.

He tears off a bit of bread. He feeds it to her. She laughs.

It's really good.

STEVE. I know.

KATE (*eating more*). You're a really good baker.

STEVE. Thanks.

KATE. Hang on. Don't look a minute. (*Turns away, takes out her bra inserts, turns back.*) Okay. This is the real me.

STEVE. They really do look like chicken fillets.

KATE. You can get them with nipples on, but I think that's a bit much. I'd feel a bit self-conscious, looking permanently perky, you know, at the post office or the bank or – do I talk too much?

STEVE. No…

KATE. I do. My parents never talked. Not to each other. So I would just fill up the silences. I kept them together for years just by *talking*. Sometimes I just want someone to interrupt me.

He kisses her. She kisses back. He stops.

STEVE. I'm sorry, was that…? Did you mean me to… you said to interrupt but…

KATE. Yes!

They kiss again.

Scene Five

They put their coats back on. We are back where we started, outside a bar on a winter evening, with music drifting out on to the alleyway and STEVE *holding out the ring to* KATE.

KATE. I feel like: nothing changes, we go down the same tracks, we find out why we're messed up and we go on doing it anyway. And apologies don't change a thing.

STEVE. I thought you wanted something different from what you've had before.

KATE. I do, I do. I never thought I could go out with someone like you – you're a vegetarian. You own a darning mushroom. You should hear my dad on the subject of your darning mushroom.

STEVE. I want to rescue you from all of that.

KATE. My knight in shining armour.

STEVE. No, I didn't mean…

KATE. I know what you mean.

STEVE. Dance with me.

KATE. You don't dance.

STEVE. I know, but dance with me.

They dance. A moment.

You see. People do change.

KATE. Are you dancing with me to prove a point?

STEVE. No… but yes.

She pulls away.

I want to.

To prove it, he carries on dancing on his own.

KATE. I want to.

STEVE. Did you – was that a yes?

KATE. Yeah.

STEVE. Really?

KATE. Yes!

STEVE. Here, wait, let me…

He puts the ring on her finger.

KATE. Oh wow.

STEVE. Is it okay?

KATE. It fits!

STEVE. Do you like it?

KATE. I love it. I love you.

STEVE. I love you too.

ACT TWO

Scene One

A few days later. KATE *is at a café with her father* JOE. *He is played by the actor playing* STEVE. *He gives her a carrier bag.*

JOE. Go on, open it.

KATE. What is it?

JOE. Have a look!

KATE. Dad.

JOE. Go on!

KATE. Dad, are you happy I'm engaged?

JOE. What?

KATE. You haven't said anything!

JOE. Of course I'm happy.

KATE. Good.

JOE. You took long enough! You made me wait! I thought I wouldn't live to dance at your wedding!

KATE. Dad…

JOE. I hope Steve knows what he's letting himself in for!

KATE. Dad!

JOE. Open the bag.

She opens the bag. She takes out a wedding veil, yellowed with age.

KATE. Is this Mum's?

JOE. My darling. You'll look just as beautiful as her. The only thing is I don't know where she put the dress. I looked all over the attic.

KATE. You don't think I'm going to wear it?

JOE. Don't say no without trying it! You can bleach it back to white.

KATE. It's bad luck.

JOE. Why?

KATE. Dad, you got divorced.

JOE. When she wore this, we were happy. Everyone said so. You could see it in her eyes.

KATE. How can you still love her after she left you like that?

JOE. You never stop loving someone. That's love, real love. You should know that if you're getting married. Love goes on forever. Till you die.

KATE (*rattled*). I do know about love.

JOE. So ask your mum if she's got the dress.

KATE. She hasn't got it.

JOE. How do you know before you ask? You're such a pessimist. Just like your mother.

KATE. Look, Dad, I know she hasn't got it.

JOE. Have you asked?

KATE. No. And I'm not wearing it anyway. Let's change the subject.

JOE. But where's the dress? It was beautiful, you know. She looked like a dream.

KATE. You'll get upset.

JOE. What's to get upset about? Kate? What is it? If you know something, tell me!

KATE. Okay. There is no dress. I came home one day after school and she was burning it. She made a little fire on the patio. The fabric went up like paper and then there was this horrid plastic thread and that just melted into a ball. You saw the pile of ash when you came home and we just said we had a barbecue and you were annoyed because you liked barbecues.

JOE. There's still a stain on that patio.

KATE. I didn't want to tell you. But now you know. So let's put this in the bin, because I'm not going to wear it.

JOE. What's the matter with you? First you burn your mother's wedding dress, now you want to throw the veil in the bin?

KATE. *She* burned her dress.

JOE. You helped.

KATE. I was fifteen!

JOE. You were the one who brought home all those feminist books. You were the one who told her about burning bras. Burning dresses maybe also! Where did she get these ideas? From you!

KATE. I stayed with you, didn't I? She said I could live with her but I stayed with you. You wouldn't have coped on your own. You could only cook scrambled eggs with spring onions. And you can't survive on scrambled eggs with spring onions.

JOE. You can't cook either.

KATE. I know, but I was *there*.

JOE. You don't even put in the spring onions.

KATE. I *stayed*. Dad.

Beat.

JOE. You're a good girl. I'm sorry. It was just a shock.

KATE. I know. I didn't want to tell you.

JOE. So I've been thinking about venues. They just built this new hall in Hendon. Your auntie says it's very nice.

KATE. Hendon?

JOE. Don't say no before you see it. Where does your mum want you to have the wedding?

KATE. I don't know.

JOE. You haven't asked her? She's the mother of the bride.

KATE. I didn't ask her. I discussed it with her. Like I'm discussing it with you. We're trying to keep everyone happy, but it's our wedding.

JOE. Hendon is very convenient. And they have their own car park.

KATE. We're having it at Greenham Common.

JOE (*laughs*). You're joking.

KATE. It's not like it sounds. They planted wildflowers, the barbed wire's gone.

JOE. It's not even in London. What if it rains?

KATE. There's this company. They do a circle of yurts.

JOE. What is a yurt?

KATE. It's a big tent, it's Mexican. Or Mongolian. Or one of those places.

JOE. Where does Steve get these ideas?

KATE. I know it's not conventional but the yurts look amazing. Really romantic, and they have these wood-burners –

JOE. Is he going to let you wear a white dress at least?

KATE. It's not about him *letting* me.

JOE. I don't want to give you away in jeans.

KATE. Okay, Dad, hang on a minute, because we really need to talk about this properly.

JOE. You should wear dresses more. And heels. You should wear heels. Then you look like a woman. You look nice.

KATE. Dad, we don't want you to give me away.

JOE. What?

KATE. It implies I'm your property.

JOE. But it's part of the ceremony.

KATE. We'll find you something else to do in the wedding, something meaningful.

JOE. I don't want to do something else. It's a tradition and it's beautiful and all my life I dreamed of going for that walk with you. But if you don't want it, good luck to you.

KATE. Dad, I love you. I want you to dance at my wedding. Will you do that for me?

JOE. It's Steve, isn't it. He's so different.

KATE. He's not really…

JOE. He's not like us.

KATE. They really care about feminism a lot.

JOE. I don't mean that.

KATE. What do you mean?

JOE. I mean he's not Jewish.

KATE. Oh, Dad, I'm sorry. I know that's important to you but I was always going to marry someone I loved no matter what his religion. You know that.

JOE. I know.

KATE. Don't be upset.

JOE. I'm not upset. I'm just glad you're getting married after all these years! I'm happy you're marrying a man. Any man!

KATE. Dad!

JOE. You know what? Tell him, fine, my dad won't give me away, but I'm wearing my mother's veil.

KATE. But I don't want to wear Mum's veil.

JOE. I'm teaching you about negotiation. You can't just cut your roots. This is where you come from. And your mother was happy when she wore this. I know. I was there.

Scene Two

That evening. STEVE *and* MORAG *are at her place. She is wearing a holey jumper. She is played by the actor playing* KATE.

MORAG. I'm sorry I haven't cooked. I got caught up. It's a shame because you should see the allotment. I cooked this fennel the other night that tasted so much of itself it was incredible. Why didn't you and Kate come together?

STEVE. I wanted to tell you myself.

MORAG. Break the news.

STEVE. No.

MORAG. Soften me up.

STEVE. No. Mum!

MORAG. It's a joke. Don't be so sensitive.

STEVE. I've got champagne.

MORAG. Good.

STEVE. She'll be here soon.

MORAG. Great.

STEVE. I can do your jumper if you want.

He gets out a darning mushroom and some wool.

MORAG. Are you ashamed of me?

STEVE. What?

MORAG. You didn't do the apology, did you? You just proposed. You didn't do what we discussed.

STEVE. What's that got to do with your jumper?

MORAG. You never had a problem with how I look before.

STEVE. I just noticed last time and I got the wool; it's no trouble.

MORAG. It troubles me.

STEVE. But why?

MORAG. She's changing you, and I don't like it.

STEVE. It's got nothing to do with Kate. I just know it's your favourite, and I got the wool. It's not like I'm asking *you* to darn my socks.

MORAG. Did you apologise?

STEVE. Yes.

MORAG. And what did she say?

STEVE. It was maybe a bit much.

MORAG. Was it.

STEVE. A bit overwhelming.

MORAG. That apology was a beautiful thing. It was important.

STEVE. I know, and she got that.

MORAG. But?

STEVE. But nothing. I did the apology. She said yes.

MORAG. You know me: I can't see something wrong and not shout about it. And I've been holding my tongue because you've got to make your own mistakes, but it's one thing to let you eat a manky bit of carrot off the kitchen floor: this is your life. This is forever.

STEVE. Did you just compare my fiancée to a manky bit of carrot on a kitchen floor?

MORAG. Don't be so literal, Steve.

STEVE. We never even had a kitchen floor. We lived in a tent.

MORAG. You make so much of growing up at Greenham Common. You were only there at weekends. You were at your dad's.

STEVE. I wanted to be with you.

MORAG. You loved his place – central heating, school uniform, that barmaid cooking you fish fingers.

STEVE. They're married now, Mum. You've got to stop calling her that.

MORAG. You were so conventional. You still are. Look at you; this is the second time you've gone and got some blood diamond and entered into a slave-contract property agreement.

STEVE. I want to stand up in front of everyone and say I love her, make a promise. And the diamond's ethical.

MORAG. At least Carina was like us. This one is different.

STEVE. She's got a name!

MORAG. You tested her and she failed.

STEVE. It wasn't a test.

MORAG. What was it then?

Beat.

STEVE. She's come a long way. You'll see when you meet her dad.

MORAG. I'm not entirely looking forward to that.

STEVE. He grew up at a refugee camp. He's had a tough life. He's –

MORAG. Please don't say 'old-fashioned'.

STEVE. I'm just saying, Kate's had a lot to get past. And she's trying. And I want you to get on.

MORAG. You're definitely doing this then?

STEVE. Mum! Yes, I'm definitely doing it. I'm in love with her. And guess what: we're going to have the wedding at the Common.

MORAG. Are you really?

STEVE. We went the other day. The sun was setting, and it was like when Dad used to drop me off on Friday nights, and I'd race out of the car, do you remember? I'd see you and I'd run, and you'd lift me up and stand me on the table and you'd paint my face, first thing, you'd paint the peace sign on my face.

MORAG. You had that caterpillar sleeping bag.

STEVE. You had a poncho.

MORAG. You remember that?

STEVE. It was in those awful seventies colours. Garish orange, muddy brown. I wouldn't darn that if you asked me to.

MORAG. If you're not careful, I'll dig it out and wear it for your fiancée.

STEVE. You will be nice, won't you?

MORAG. Of course I'll be nice. Get the glasses from the dresser. They're all dusty. I'll wash, you dry. I'm your best friend.

STEVE. I know.

Scene Three

KATE *and* STEVE*, a few days later. They're at home, armed with a laptop. They do rock, paper, scissors.* KATE *wins.*

KATE. Yay! Paper covers rock!

STEVE. Fine. We'll hire a photographer.

KATE. No embarrassing poses, I promise!

STEVE. It's fine. You won. Paper covers rock.

KATE. What we really need to talk about is numbers. Dad says: he's chartering a coach from Golders and he needs to know what size. A forty-seater or a sixty-seater.

STEVE. Well, it's great that he's got so many friends.

KATE. We don't have room for them. We'll have to say no. And I already feel guilty about letting him down.

STEVE. Why? He's been wanting you to get married all your life. He should be over the moon.

KATE. Because this isn't his dream wedding. I burst into tears in the dress shop.

STEVE. Don't tell me about the dress!

KATE. I won't but you'll laugh: they had this diagram on the wall. How to use a bin bag to go to the loo.

STEVE. Can we talk about confetti now?

KATE. Too much information?

STEVE. It's bad luck. And everything's so beautiful. And I don't want my happiness to end.

KATE (*kisses him*). Okay. No more dress talk. And I'm up for confetti.

STEVE. So my mum called about it, and actually I agree with her. She wants ethical confetti.

KATE. As opposed to devious confetti?

STEVE. As opposed to filling up some landfill site with soggy paper.

KATE. What's ethical confetti made of?

STEVE. Rose petals. Or delphiniums.

KATE. Let's do that!

STEVE. Roses or delphiniums?

KATE. Roses!

STEVE. Right.

KATE. No, wait, delphiniums!

STEVE. Okay.

KATE. Both?

STEVE. Both!

KATE. Honestly, if it was just you and me, we could plan this wedding in an hour. We could do it over a bottle of wine.

STEVE. If it was just you and me it wouldn't be a wedding.

KATE. I know. I do want it to be about building a future and a family and a community. I just wish they'd all back off.

STEVE. Now music.

KATE. I'm not walking down the aisle to '99 Red Balloons'.

STEVE. It's my favourite song.

KATE. I don't know why.

STEVE. It's about nuclear disarmament.

KATE. It's not romantic.

STEVE. It *is*.

KATE. Not happy-romantic though!

STEVE. Well what do you want?

KATE. 'I Need a Hero'!

STEVE. Okay…

KATE. No! Don't do rock paper scissors. That's not my choice. Once you've done rock paper scissors it's sacred. Let's think of songs we really want.

STEVE. I can only think of inappropriate ones now…

KATE. Me too.

STEVE. 'I Still Haven't Found What I'm Looking For'.

KATE. 'Will You Still Love Me Tomorrow?'

STEVE. 'Love Will Tear Us Apart'.

KATE. No, wait! Here's a real one: Kate Bush. 'Wuthering Heights'. I come down the aisle wanting to be let in at your window and, you're going to love this: you whip out a window frame, and then you say 'Okay' and you *open the window* and I climb through. And it's like: I have broken that pattern. I have come inside.

STEVE. Then I want the Robin Hood theme song.

KATE. That Bryan Adams song? *Seriously?* You have a heart of cheese.

STEVE. No. You know, the one about him riding through the glen.

KATE. You're joking.

STEVE. It is how we met.

KATE. No way.

STEVE. Rock, paper, scissors. Let's go.

KATE. That's your actual choice? Fine.

They do rock, paper, scissors. STEVE *wins.*

STEVE. Rock blunts scissors!

KATE. No!

STEVE. Sorry. Once you've done rock paper scissors it's sacred.

KATE. I hate you right now, you know that.

STEVE. I know. Now what about cake toppers?

KATE (*sulking*). I don't want little people on top of the cake.

STEVE. Look what we can get though. We can get a bride and groom high-fiving each other.

KATE. In tiny plastic. Weird. And no.

STEVE. Me squeezing your arse.

KATE. No!

STEVE. You squeezing mine.

KATE. Definitely not. Oh my God. That couple's shagging on the cake. That's not even hygienic. These are the least romantic things I've ever seen.

They see one they both like.

STEVE. Look.

KATE. That's just…

STEVE. That's perfect.

He takes her hand. Unconsciously they have assumed the pose of a traditional bride and groom on the top of a cake.

Scene shifts: it is now the day of STEVE *and* KATE*'s wedding, a summer's day a few months on. They are getting dressed. He shuts his eyes because he's superstitious about looking at her dress. They giggle as he feels his way to do up her dress. She pins on his buttonhole, swiftly and expertly. She puts on her mother's veil. She sprays perfume in front of herself and jumps into it.*

There are cheers, and confetti showers the stage. They kiss, to more cheering. They are married.

A series of clicks as they pose for photographs, including:

holding hands

sticking their tongues out at each other

holding up an old gilt picture frame with them inside it

wearing false moustaches

wearing animal masks

kissing

They exit. This is the first time both have left the stage in the play.

Scene Four

It is later that evening; music drifts through from the wedding party, just offstage. A meadow covered with wildflowers: Greenham Common. JOE *enters. He is about to drink some whisky when* MORAG *enters.*

JOE. Whisky?

MORAG. Always.

He pours her an enormous shot.

JOE. L'chaim.

MORAG. You're a long time dead.

They drink.

JOE. No one's dancing!

MORAG. Steve did the first dance. He's shown willing.

JOE. One dance? This is supposed to be a party.

MORAG. He doesn't like dancing.

JOE. Everyone likes dancing.

MORAG. Not my son.

JOE. Do you like dancing?

MORAG. Yes.

JOE. You see?

MORAG (*laughs*). Fill me up.

He pours.

JOE. Those speeches!

MORAG. Yes!

JOE. So serious! Who died?

MORAG. So *long*.

JOE. Why talk about forced marriage? It makes us look bad.

MORAG. Yes and I feel as strongly about genetically modified corn as the next woman but there are times and places.

JOE. They should have let me make a speech. I even had a joke. Do you want to hear it?

MORAG. Go on.

JOE. 'This is such an emotional wedding. Even the cake's in tiers.' Huh?

MORAG. Don't give up the day job. What is your day job again?

JOE. Import export.

MORAG. Are you an arms dealer?

JOE. No! I do novelty telephones. Duck phones, frog phones, teddy-bear phones… ducks are our biggest seller. The British are obsessed by ducks.

MORAG. Really?

JOE. We've got three duck phones – Quacky One, Quacky Two and Quacky Three. One's a girl duck, one's a boy duck and the other's a, you know, the grey ones; what do you call them?

MORAG (*laughs*). Canada goose!

JOE. Canada goose. People also like the hamburger phone. But in my opinion, it's not very comfortable. The gherkins get stuck in your ears.

They look back towards the wedding.

MORAG. Has that rabbi got food in his beard?

JOE. What do you want? It's not easy to get a rabbi to bless a goy who hasn't had the snip.

MORAG. Did you actually just call it 'the snip'?

JOE. I'm happy Steve let a rabbi do the blessing. He did a nice job.

MORAG. He did.

JOE. I don't know what happened with the glass. It usually breaks just like that.

MORAG. I think it was the napkin. It was too thick. It did smash; you just couldn't hear it.

JOE. I never saw a groom have a problem before. It's not even a glass, you know, it's a lightbulb. It should be easy. Just put your foot down and bang. They say it's the last time the man gets to put his foot down.

MORAG. That isn't seriously the tradition? Steve didn't just –

JOE. No, no. It's a joke. It's to show the fragility of life. We don't know what will happen. Even when we are happy there is pain. And… I have a stone in my shoe. Take that a second… (*Hands her the whisky, and gets the stone out of the shoe*.) Oof, that's better. Thank you. (*Takes back the whisky*.) Who gets married outside? I haven't slept in a tent since the refugee camp. When we got our flat in Tel Aviv, I made a resolution I would always have a floor. A man should have a floor. But how many daughters do I have?

MORAG. It's going to be beautiful when the sun comes up.

JOE. It's going to be cold.

MORAG. How long were you at that refugee camp?

JOE. Six years.

MORAG. That's how long I was here, on the Common.

JOE (*tops up her drink*). Here. It'll keep you warm.

MORAG. I don't get cold.

JOE. I feel cold just looking at you. Take my jacket.

MORAG. No, thanks.

JOE. Take it, take it!

MORAG (*not taking it*). No thanks. You're very direct.

JOE. I'm very Israeli. L'chaim.

They drink.

My mouth's still slimy from the cake.

MORAG. Steve made that cake with love.

JOE. Did he have to make it out of avocado?

MORAG. They have a lot of vegan friends. Did Kate have to wear a veil?

JOE. She looked perfect.

MORAG. That veil symbolises her hymen.

JOE. I'm not naive. I know she's not a virgin.

MORAG. That's not why I've got a problem with it.

JOE. She's been around the block. I know.

MORAG. That's not what's bothering me.

JOE. Many blocks.

MORAG. When you lift the veil it symbolises the breaking of the hymen. Doesn't that strike you as weird? At a public event? In front of friends and family?

JOE. You feminists. You make everything about sex.

MORAG. Everything is already about sex.

JOE. Even this conversation?

MORAG. No. Not this conversation.

Beat.

JOE. I just think feminism's gone too far.

MORAG. What? Why?

JOE. Look at my wife: most women love babies, but she was crying all the time, she stopped washing her hair, she kept saying she was bored.

MORAG. Babies are boring.

JOE. Then Kate starts bringing home these books, feminist books. She and my wife sit in the kitchen talking, talking. I come home, they go quiet. My wife says I'm like Hitler. How can I be like Hitler? I'm a bloody Jew. She says keep your voice down. How can I help my voice?

MORAG. Yes, how can you help anything? How can you help you're white and middle class and male and straight and able-bodied.

JOE. It's not my fault you're not a man!

MORAG. I don't want to be a man!

JOE. These feminists get ideas and take them to extremes. All ideas are bad if you go to extremes.

MORAG. How has feminism gone to extremes? We don't even have equal pay yet!

JOE. You lived in a tent for six years! For your ideas! That's extreme!

MORAG. I was fighting for our children's *lives*.

JOE. You're so lucky; you're born here; the weather's moderate, the politics are moderate, you're safe, but you make yourself like a person in the Third World, and for what?

MORAG. For world peace.

JOE. You sound like a beauty queen. World peace.

MORAG. We got those missiles out. We won.

JOE. You think you saved the world by going camping? The missiles went because of Gorbachev.

MORAG. I did six years in mud and filth to get those missiles out. You should be grateful.

JOE. You didn't do it for me. You just said why you did it: Steve was boring.

She slaps him. A moment. He laughs.

MORAG. Don't laugh!

JOE. A woman never hit me before.

MORAG. I've never hit anyone before. I'm sorry. Really. That was totally uncalled for. Are you all right?

JOE. I'm fine! I barely felt it.

MORAG. I just had no idea I was going to do that.

JOE. I did.

MORAG. Why?

JOE. You hate men, why shouldn't you hit us?

MORAG. I don't hate men.

JOE. When was the last time you were with a man?

MORAG. That's none of your business.

JOE. So it's been a long time.

MORAG. We're going to be related. I don't want to do anything else I regret here. I'm going back inside.

JOE. Don't. I don't understand anyone in there. I should have chartered that coach and brought some people I could talk to. I can talk to you. Stay a minute. Tell me what it was like when you were here before.

MORAG. There was a big fence over there and a load of missiles on the other side of it. That's what it was like.

JOE. What was it like for you? What did you do, all that time? You must have done something in six years.

MORAG. We knitted, we made lots of tea, nuns brought us raisins. Once, we dressed up as teddy bears. We covered ourselves with honey so we'd be too sticky for the soldiers to move us on.

JOE. They must have loved that – a bunch of naked women covered in honey?

MORAG. We were in bear costumes.

JOE. Oh I thought –

MORAG. I know what you thought. We didn't wear earrings, especially not dangly earrings; a man could grab those and pull and you can't imagine how much blood comes out of an ear. We cut the fence. We went to prison. We came out. We cut the fence again. We shaved our heads so we didn't have to wash our hair. We ate apples so we didn't have to brush our teeth. We felt raw all the time, and alive; up against it, surviving.

JOE. And after that, nothing else feels like real life.

MORAG (*surprised*). Yes. You're right.

JOE. It was hot at the refugee camp. The sun was so bright, we'd get up at six in the morning. I stole oranges from the groves. My mother put the blossoms in her hair. We danced around the fires in the evenings. All the songs were new. (*Looks back at the wedding*.) That husband of yours is an idiot. To go from you to that woman? She's got no sense of humour, no spirit, nothing.

MORAG. Maybe after me that's what he wanted.

JOE. Like I said: an idiot. And did you see my wife? I went right up to her, tears in my eyes. Our daughter just got married. And she turned her face.

MORAG. I wish my ex would blank me. It's better than having to talk to that barmaid.

JOE. It isn't better, believe me.

Beat.

MORAG. You know why we broke up? It was stupid. I lost my wedding ring. He said I must have put it on the fence. A lot of women put stuff on the fence. But I didn't. It was so cold, your fingers shrink. I didn't even notice it fall off. But he didn't believe me. He thought I didn't care.

JOE. You're so sad. I've never seen anyone as sad as you.

MORAG. I've reason to be.

JOE. Dance with me.

MORAG. What? No.

JOE. It's a wedding. The parents of the couple dance. It's normal!

MORAG. I'm not dancing with you.

JOE. I do ceroc. I'm very good.

MORAG. You think if we dance, you'll win.

JOE. I just thought it would be nice! You think too much.

MORAG. If we don't think, we're just animals.

JOE. We are just animals. We have needs, we have desires. It's my daughter's wedding, I want to dance. Come on. Give me that.

She lets him take her drink. He puts it down next to the bottle.

MORAG. I don't think it's a good idea.

JOE. Ssshhhh, don't think.

MORAG. Don't silence me.

JOE. Did I use force? Did I do anything bad?

MORAG. No…

JOE. Sshhhhh…. (*Puts his finger to his lips.*) We can both be quiet, yes?

MORAG. Yes.

They start to dance. They dance close.

JOE. I told you I was good.

They kiss. She breaks away.

MORAG. It's our children's wedding.

JOE. Sssssshhhh.

MORAG. It's completely wrong.

JOE. Please.

MORAG. I don't care, I don't care about anything. Kiss me again.

They kiss again. They start ripping off each other's clothes…

As they do, they are now no longer JOE *and* MORAG*, but* STEVE *and* KATE. (STEVE *and* KATE*'s wedding outfits are revealed underneath* JOE *and* MORAG*'s.*)

They have walked in on their parents. And they are panicking.

KATE. Oh fuck.

STEVE. Kate.

KATE. Fuck.

STEVE. Where did they go?

KATE. I don't know!

STEVE. Should we go after them?

KATE. No. *No*.

STEVE. You're right.

KATE. Oh God.

STEVE. Let's just, let's just talk about it.

KATE. I don't want to talk about it! I don't think we should talk about it!

STEVE. We have to talk about it!

KATE. Why?

STEVE. Because it happened!

KATE. Lots of things happen we don't talk about. Babies born in China! Every minute there's a baby born in China and you never say, I never say, you know what, just now, over in Beijing –

STEVE. We can't not talk about it!

KATE. Yes we can. We can never talk about it, ever. We can just decide.

STEVE. We can't!

KATE. Rock, paper, scissors?

STEVE. No!

KATE. It's the fairest way!

STEVE. If we don't talk about it, something really bad will happen.

KATE. Something really bad has happened.

STEVE. Let's think this through.

KATE. No!

STEVE. We can't pretend it never happened.

KATE. Yes we can.

STEVE. Christmas will be awkward. Chanukah.

KATE. *Chanukah?*

STEVE. You need to talk to your dad. You need to find him and tell him he's out of line.

KATE. And you find your mum, and tell her?

STEVE. No, it's him we need to talk to.

KATE. They were both here!

STEVE. My mum didn't start it.

KATE. How do you know?

STEVE. There's no way she'd be attracted to him!

KATE. Did you *see* her?

STEVE. I saw *him*.

KATE. What's that supposed to mean?

STEVE. He was pulling her hair.

KATE. People do sometimes! It doesn't mean anything.

STEVE. I should've decked him. I should go and find him now and –

KATE. She looked like she was having fun.

STEVE. Bollocks.

KATE. Are you saying he forced her?

STEVE. No.

KATE. Really?

STEVE. I'm not saying that.

KATE. Because it sounded a lot like –

STEVE. He just *takes*! Like it's his right. He thinks everyone's fair game, even my mum.

KATE. You've got this massive blind spot about your mum and you just don't see: she was there too!

STEVE. She didn't want it. And even if she did, she wouldn't have done it. She's not like him just taking, taking, taking, not like him, not thinking, not considering, just grabbing what he wants.

KATE. What's wrong with grabbing what you want sometimes?

STEVE. It's selfish. It's completely wrong!

KATE. At least it's honest. Sometimes I wish you'd turn your head off, grab what you want.

STEVE. You don't.

KATE. Sometimes I wish you'd make decisions, choose wine, open doors, drive a car, operate a drill – eat steak! Be a bit more rapey when we go to bed. (*Quickly covers her mouth.*) I didn't mean that. Steve. I didn't mean to say that.

STEVE. But you did.

KATE. It just came out my mouth. It isn't what I mean.

STEVE. I thought you'd changed.

KATE. I have.

STEVE. You want me to eat steak?

KATE. I don't.

STEVE. You're a vegetarian.

KATE. I know.

STEVE. You've been a vegetarian for eighteen years.

KATE. I know!

STEVE. You want me to be 'rapey'?

KATE. I hate this, I didn't want to talk. You want to talk. Don't yell at me for using the wrong words.

STEVE. It's repulsive. To use a cutesy diminutive for the most violent, revolting act.

KATE. You say you could murder a drink.

STEVE. You're the one. You're the one who says. You haven't changed.

KATE. I have, I have. You've got to trust me.

STEVE. You're not the person I thought you were.

KATE. This is why we shouldn't talk. We're making it worse. Let's get some more to drink. Let's find them if we have to. I'd rather stick pins in my eyes but if you want to; Steve? You're not saying anything. Don't give me the silent treatment. Not *now*. You're the one who wanted to talk. I'm talking. Steve.

STEVE. I think I'm going to leave. I think I have to go.

KATE. Go where?

STEVE. Just go.

KATE. What do you mean, just go?

STEVE. Leave. Leave you.

KATE. What do you mean, leave? We're fucking married now.

STEVE (*checks his watch*). For ninety minutes.

KATE. Did you just check your watch to see how long we're married?

STEVE. I'm sorry.

KATE. This is supposed to be the happiest day of my life.

STEVE. I'm sorry.

He starts to exit.

KATE. Stop saying that. You can't. Steve. You can't.

He's gone. She looks stunned.

Steve? Steve?

Pause. She grabs a microphone.

STEVE!

The party noises go silent. STEVE *has gone. She looks at the microphone in her hand. And then at her guests.*

This isn't a speech. This isn't a wedding. Steve's gone. But don't you go! There's champagne. Cake. You can have your presents back. We won't need the three-bin recycling centre or the sherry schooners or the cake slide that says 'love laughter and happy ever after'. The sheep for the African village and the revolving ram; that's up to your own conscience. I'm sorry. I just want this dress I want it off I want it gone I want it in the fire. I'm burning it. It's going in that fucking wood-burner.

Blackout.

Scene Five

Two days later. STEVE *is at* MORAG*'s flat. He's dishevelled, drunk, and still in his wedding gear.*

STEVE. Mum.

MORAG. I'll put on some coffee. I'll run you a bath.

STEVE. No but there must be whisky.

MORAG. How could you be so thoughtless?

STEVE. Me?

MORAG. I'd best call Kate and Joe. Let them know you're alive. You're going to have to face the music.

STEVE. How could *I* be thoughtless?

MORAG. It's been two days.

STEVE. How could you get together with that misogynist pig, Mum?

MORAG. Steve!

STEVE. Sorry. Do we need a lawyer?

MORAG. A lawyer?

STEVE. Did he hurt you?

MORAG. No.

STEVE. Did he force you? Push you into it?

MORAG. Of course not!

STEVE. Are you sure?

MORAG. Yes! Listen. I'm sorry it happened at your wedding, I'm sorry you saw it, it must have been very upsetting, but –

STEVE. He's everything we hate.

MORAG. Yes well he's been worried sick. Driving up and down the motorway, looking for you.

STEVE. He hates women.

MORAG. You need to calm down.

STEVE. You teach me to be respectful, to think before I act, you make me be this *lovely person*. Then you go off with this woman-hater.

MORAG. You're shouting.

STEVE. You're sleeping with the enemy.

MORAG. Lower your voice.

STEVE. I've been lowering my voice for years! I've tied myself in knots, trying to be the best male feminist there is. Carina dumps me. Kate wants me to 'eat steak'. Now you! You're all the same. Women. You all want the same thing.

Beat.

MORAG. Do we.

STEVE. What other conclusion can I draw?

MORAG. I'm not just your mother. I have desires. I want things. You weren't supposed to see. You were supposed to be on the dance floor. I know he's your father-in-law, I know I can't have him. But you're talking like I can't have anyone.

STEVE. I thought you were happy being single.

MORAG. I've been alone a really long time.

STEVE. So go out with someone nice. Find a feminist.

MORAG. There's no such thing.

STEVE. What?

MORAG. There's no such thing as a male feminist.

STEVE (*stunned*). Of course there is.

MORAG. Look at you, even you; you've been shouting, looming over me.

STEVE. I'm sorry, I'm upset, I didn't mean –

MORAG. You'll never know how it feels. You'll never really understand.

STEVE. But I want to. Mum.

MORAG. It's not always about what you want. Is it.

STEVE. But Mum. (*Retches.*) Sorry. (*Retches.*)

MORAG. Are you all right?

STEVE. I haven't slept. I don't think I've really slept.

MORAG. I'll get you a glass of water.

STEVE. I spent last night in a doorway. I think I ate a burger. From a van. What am I going to do? Mum? I wish you'd tell me what to do. I don't know what I've done.

MORAG. Steve. (*Puts her arms around him.*) It's all right.

STEVE. It really isn't.

MORAG. It'll be all right.

He breaks the hug.

STEVE. No, I feel sick. My head is spinning.

MORAG. Sit down. Put your head between your legs. Or maybe not if you feel sick. Sit down.

STEVE (*gets out his phone*). I don't want to turn this on. (*Turns it on, watches the screen, waiting for it to start up. It starts to beep. There are a lot of messages.*) Kate. Kate. Kate. Joe. Kate. You. Kate. Kate. Carina. Kate. Joe.

MORAG. Leave it.

STEVE. But I have to…

MORAG. They've waited two days, they can wait another hour. Come on now. Coffee. Bath. No whisky. Toast. All right? And then we'll see.

ACT THREE

Scene One

Six weeks later. Another fancy-dress party at Jenny's. Music drifts in from the house. STEVE *is there, dressed as John Stuart Mill in a frock coat and cravat. It's hot. He fans himself with his top hat.* CARINA *arrives, with drinks, in the cat ears from before.*

CARINA. Roman slave girl.

STEVE. You're joking.

CARINA. Jenny says that's how women dressed in Imperial Rome. According to the internet.

STEVE. I can see her lunch.

CARINA. I hate fancy dress.

STEVE. Well I feel ridiculous. And hot. And everyone thinks I'm Charles Dickens.

CARINA. I know who you are.

STEVE. Because it was your idea.

CARINA. You look good as John Stuart Mill.

STEVE. No one knows who he is. I have to keep giving them the lecture.

CARINA. They should be glad of the education. The first male feminist should be better known.

STEVE. Why do you hate fancy dress?

CARINA. It feels like lying. I don't like games either. Or *banter*. I don't like anything where you make things up and pretend you're something you're not.

STEVE. You don't want to be mysterious?

CARINA. Why would I want to do that?

STEVE. Kate said women like being mysterious.

CARINA. Kate does not speak for all women.

STEVE. She'd love this costume. I look just like Heathcliff.

CARINA. She's not invited.

STEVE. I know. I checked with Jenny.

CARINA. You still haven't seen her?

STEVE. I can't.

CARINA. You don't need to. You owe her nothing.

STEVE. Well…

CARINA. It drives me mad the way everyone's tiptoeing round it. Why can't we all just admit she wasn't worthy of you. She never got how brilliant you are. I mean, you're like an advert for what happens when a feminist has a son. You prove: men have changed. Men are better!

STEVE. You make me sound like a prototype.

CARINA. You are! I mean, you're not, of course. You're you and you're wonderful.

STEVE. Do you think men can be feminists?

CARINA. Yes.

STEVE. I don't mean fellow travellers, I mean really in our hearts.

CARINA. Look, your mum said you went round and got a bit shouty. But of course you're a feminist. What else are you?

STEVE. I don't know.

CARINA. Trust me, you're a feminist.

STEVE. You're so certain. How are you so certain?

CARINA. You worry too much.

STEVE. I know.

CARINA. I'm glad you came out tonight. It's been six weeks. You can't just mope.

STEVE. Thanks for making me come.

CARINA. Any time. (*Beat.*) Do you ever worry about us? That we did the wrong thing?

STEVE. That wasn't my decision.

CARINA. But you must have thought about it.

STEVE. It's a long time ago.

CARINA. It isn't really.

STEVE. I'm really glad we're friends.

CARINA. Steve, do you still feel for me?

STEVE. What?

CARINA. The other day at the allotment I took my jumper off, and your mum noticed I'm still wearing your ring. I've had it on this chain round my neck all this time. I kept meaning to give it back. I know that's the right thing to do. But I just haven't got round to it. And now I think maybe there's a reason.

STEVE. Carina, you dumped me.

CARINA. I remember.

STEVE. You said you liked the idea of me.

CARINA. I know. It was completely irrational! It was like I wanted to be swept off my feet, to have a crazy romantic love affair. And I don't want any of that. Especially now I've seen what it's done to you. I mean, you and Kate were head-over-heels in love and what a car crash! Isn't it better to base a relationship on shared ideas and mutual respect and history? And that's what we've got.

STEVE. How can you do this *now*?

CARINA. I made a mistake.

STEVE. I'm *married*.

CARINA. You made a mistake too. (*Undoing the chain, and taking off the ring.*) Look. You can have the ring back if you want. It's yours. Or I could keep it and we could decide this has been a blip and we could try again. (*Holding out the ring to him as if proposing.*) Just think about it.

STEVE. I can't do this. I can't be this fickle person.

CARINA. I'm not rushing you. I'm not going down on one knee. I'm just saying: we make sense. We agree. Maybe tomorrow you can come to the allotment. Help me and your mum with the weeding. Everything's choked. Nothing can breathe. We'll have a really good day. Don't make any decisions now. Just think. Just think how good it could be.

Scene Two

A month later. KATE *and* ROSS. *They laugh as she is drunkenly trying to unlock the door to her flat.*

ROSS. Give me those keys. You're wasted.

KATE. You made me match you drink for drink.

ROSS. You needed cheering up.

He takes the keys from her and opens the door. They fall into the flat, laughing.

KATE. We're in!

ROSS. Right. Bed.

KATE. No, no. You have to go home.

ROSS. I live in Clapham!

KATE. So?

ROSS. I'm not getting a cab across the river. And two old friends can share a bed, can't we?

KATE. No. We can't.

ROSS. Why are you so stubborn?

KATE. I've got my reasons. I can't tell you.

ROSS. You can't tell me why you're so stubborn?

KATE. I can't tell you why we can't share a bed – you'll laugh.

ROSS. I won't.

KATE. You will.

ROSS. I'll be very serious. This is my serious face.

KATE. I'll repulse you.

ROSS. Have you developed scales? In your ten weeks of spinsterhood. Do you have gills? What *is* it?

KATE. I didn't shave my legs.

ROSS (*laughs*). Is that all?

KATE. I told you you'd laugh.

ROSS. This isn't a feminist thing, is it? I thought you were over that.

KATE. I'm over Steve. I'm not over wanting equality.

ROSS. Tell me you've done your pits.

KATE. It was so this wouldn't happen.

ROSS. What?

KATE. This. You coming back with me. So I wouldn't be tempted. To let anything happen.

ROSS. Nothing's happening, babes. I'm just putting a drunk married lady to bed.

KATE. Okay.

ROSS. Unless of course you want something to happen…

He pulls back her hair and kisses her hard. She shoves him away and wipes her mouth.

KATE. Get off!

ROSS. Don't wipe your mouth.

KATE. Don't pull my hair.

ROSS. I know what you like.

KATE. You have to *ask*.

ROSS. Ask?

KATE. Yes, ask.

ROSS. Please may I pull your hair.

KATE. No you can't.

ROSS. I wasn't actually asking.

KATE. Sorry if I've spoiled your fun. You need to go.

ROSS. Not *my* fun. Sometimes for a clever person you can be very thick. Asking would ruin it for you. You want to be swept up, taken over, you want to lose yourself.

KATE. I don't, I don't.

ROSS. You're repressed. You need someone to blast through all that.

KATE. And you don't enjoy it at all.

ROSS. No. Your neuroses coincide with my sexual tastes. That's why we're so well matched.

KATE. I don't want to be neurotic.

ROSS. Tough.

KATE. I've changed.

ROSS. People don't change. We know that. We work for a newspaper. People make the same mistakes over and over and sometimes they enjoy them.

KATE. I have changed. I have. I have been with someone *nice*.

ROSS. Oh please. You're the same you've always been. And all this fretting over who you are is so decadent. It's changing deckchairs on the *Titanic*.

KATE. What's the iceberg?

ROSS. The planet. We're all just animals facing starvation, and you worry about being a good feminist, a good Jew. When the time comes, you'll let someone rape you for the last bacon sandwich.

KATE. God, you're bleak.

ROSS. I'm the only one who tells you the truth. I've missed you terribly.

KATE. You see me every day at work.

ROSS. Not naked.

KATE. Aren't you seeing Jenny?

ROSS. God, no.

KATE. You said she was funny and uninhibited.

ROSS. She is. But, as previously established, I don't like uninhibited.

KATE. Are you being nice to me now?

ROSS. You know I adore you. Hell would freeze over before I'd treat a woman the way Steve's treated you.

KATE. Last night I went to the bakery and I knew he was in there; I could see the light from the ovens. But he didn't open the door.

ROSS. What a coward.

KATE. I think he's still in shock.

ROSS. After two months?

KATE. Two and a half. I miss him. I just want it to be like it was.

ROSS. He hasn't told you. Fuck. I really am the only one who tells you the truth.

KATE. What truth?

ROSS. He's getting married.

KATE. No.

ROSS. He is.

KATE. But he can't. We're still. We only just.

ROSS. I know! Jenny asked me to come as her plus one and I told her: he can't be getting married. He's still married to you. And you can't get a divorce just like that.

KATE. You have to be married a year.

ROSS. But they don't need one for this. It's some kind of pagan handfasting troth-pledging. They'll make it legal later. I'll sabotage it if you want. Piss on the cake. Spike the champagne. Punch him in the face. Don't cry.

KATE. Who's he marrying?

ROSS. Carina.

KATE. Fuck.

ROSS. I know. Don't cry. He's not worth it.

KATE. I'm fine.

ROSS. Don't be fine. Write a nasty bitter feature. Someone must have taken a picture of you stuffing your dress into that wood-burner. We'll put it on the front page of the supplement. 'My Feminist Husband Ruined My Life'. I'll give you seven thousand words.

KATE. I'm a serious journalist.

ROSS. Have my handkerchief. Don't use a tissue. You're basically rubbing wood shavings on your face. Here.

KATE. Thanks.

He wipes her eyes. He kisses the tears away. They kiss, gently this time.

ROSS. Let's go to bed. Come on. It'll be like old times. And we belong together. We're both as doomed as each other. Let me look after you.

They kiss again. But then she hiccups.

Charming.

KATE. Oh I hate hiccups. (*Hiccups again.*) They go on for hours. (*Again.*)

ROSS. Don't worry.

She gasps – ROSS *has pulled a knife on her.*

KATE. What the fuck?

ROSS. Cured you. (*Beat.*) It's only a penknife.

KATE. Are you a fucking Boy Scout?

ROSS. Scaring people to cure hiccups is a thing you do. A thing. Like putting dropped gloves on railings. Writing thank you notes. A thing.

KATE. I want you to go now.

ROSS. Come on…

KATE. I'm not doomed. I don't want to be doomed. Go away.

ROSS. But Kate –

KATE. Get out.

Scene Three

Two weeks later. KATE *and* JOE *are at a café. He brings over two cups of coffee.*

KATE. I said I don't want coffee, Dad.

JOE. So maybe you change your mind.

KATE. I won't change my mind.

JOE. It's good. They roast the beans themselves. And I'm getting you a croissant.

KATE. I don't want a croissant.

JOE. It's true, they're not as good as Steve's.

KATE (*warningly*). Dad…

JOE. I miss his croissants.

KATE. Dad!

JOE. So flaky. So much butter.

KATE. I can't deal with this, Dad. Not today. Please. He's getting married.

JOE. You didn't get through to him.

KATE. No I didn't get through to him. He's probably pinning on a buttonhole right now. Half my friends are there in fascinators cheering him on. I'm so angry I could crawl out of my skin.

JOE. It's not a real wedding.

KATE. You don't think it's real unless it's in Hendon.

JOE. No.

KATE. It's true; you don't.

JOE. I'm saying there's no registrar, no rabbi. There's not even a yurt. He broke a glass for you! That's not nothing.

KATE. Yes and in half an hour he's going to stand up in front of everyone and tell them he loves her not me so can we please not talk about it. I don't want to hear his name.

JOE (*checks his watch*). Half an hour.

KATE. Don't do that.

JOE. What?

KATE. You know what. Don't look at your watch. Just tell me when it's finished.

JOE. So it's really over, you and him.

KATE. Yes.

JOE. Finished. That's it. Kaput.

KATE. Dad!

JOE. What?

KATE. Can we please not talk about it.

JOE. Okay, fine, don't talk about it.

KATE. Thanks.

JOE. Drink your coffee.

KATE. I don't want coffee!

JOE. Just one sip!

She drinks coffee in silence. He watches her.

If it's really over with you two, I might call her.

KATE. Who?

JOE. Morag! Who?

KATE. Why would you call her?

JOE. I liked her.

KATE. You mean for a *date*?

JOE. We got on all right.

KATE. Are you mad?

JOE. We had a nice time.

KATE. She's the mother of my husband.

JOE. You were only married for an hour.

KATE. It was ninety minutes!

JOE. So anyway, you're not married now.

KATE. Yes I am! What he's doing now's not real. And she's his *mother*.

JOE. All right I won't call her.

KATE. I can't believe you'd even think about it.

JOE. Sorry for thinking!

KATE. You don't even know it's wrong, do you?

JOE. Why are you getting so upset?

KATE. I just want some loyalty. I want you on my side. I want to stop being surrounded by men who do everything they want. I want to stop feeling like this. I want – I want Steve! (*Kicks off her shoes.*)

JOE. Why are you taking off your shoes?

KATE. I can't run in heels.

JOE. Why are you running?

KATE. To get to Steve!

JOE. You haven't even got socks on.

KATE. I have to get there.

JOE. Get a taxi.

KATE. You're right.

JOE (*hits his head*). What am I, an idiot? I'll drive you!

Beat.

KATE. Give me the keys! I'll drive.

JOE (*giving her the keys*). Let's go!

Scene Four

STEVE *is in an upstairs room of a pub. He's fumbling with a buttonhole.* CARINA *enters, wearing something horrible.*

CARINA. So, do I scrub up all right?

STEVE *has covered up his eyes.*

STEVE. I can't *look*.

CARINA. Come on, we're not superstitious.

STEVE. Just humour me.

CARINA. Just look at me!

STEVE. No!

CARINA. You've made a pig's ear of that buttonhole. You don't need to wear it, you know. Not for me. This isn't formal. Not like your last wedding.

STEVE. Don't talk about my last wedding.

CARINA. You're jumpy.

STEVE. I want to do things right this time.

CARINA. Look at me then. Open your eyes. This is you and me. We know exactly who we are. No mystery. Open your eyes.

He uncovers his eyes and looks at her. And realises this is not what he wants.

STEVE. I don't like this. It's not right.

CARINA (*laughs*). It's fine. Let's go in.

STEVE. Give me a minute. (*Goes back to his buttonhole.*) I'll just…

CARINA. Ditch it. What does it matter?

STEVE. I'll follow you in.

CARINA. Do you want me to get your mum?

STEVE. My mum? No. Why?

CARINA. She'll know how to pin it on. If you're set on it. She's just outside.

STEVE (*looking anxiously at the door*). Is she?

CARINA. I'll get her.

STEVE. No! I mean it's fine. Don't worry.

CARINA. Good. I'll tell them you're on your way.

She exits.

Alone, he panics. He pulls the buttonhole off and undoes the top button of his shirt. He tries to breathe calmly. He looks wildly towards the door, as a peal of laughter comes from the other side of it.

KATE *enters through a window.*

KATE. Hi.

STEVE. How did you get in?

KATE. Fire escape. Open window.

STEVE. You can't be here.

KATE. I know it's stupid and probably wrong. I just have to tell you because in half an hour it'll be so much more stupid and wrong. Fuck it, Steve: I love you.

STEVE. This is terrible.

KATE. And I think the other men, the bad men, they were like, you know in tribes where before you get married, someone deflowers you with a stick? And then you have sex with your husband and it doesn't hurt and it's not, you know, with a stick, so you don't associate him with the pain, you can love him with your whole heart. I *do* talk too much. Run away with me.

STEVE. Now?

KATE. Before it's too late.

STEVE. Carina's out there. My *mum*'s out there.

KATE. Are you in love with her? Steve? Because I'm over Heathcliff. No, honestly. I read *Wuthering Heights* again and he hits a woman on page twenty-eight, and I don't want that! And I wish I never said that word. I've got to stop just saying stuff, I've got to *think* more. And you've got to think less! You can't make everything a test. You have to trust me a little bit. Because we're going to be together for a really long time. Because love is forever, till you die.

STEVE. I can't just walk out.

KATE. You've done it before.

STEVE. Yes and I'm not going to do it again.

KATE. Oh fuck. Fuck. I've made a horrible mistake. You don't want to run away with me.

STEVE. I don't want to run away. Come on.

He takes her hand, and before she realises it, he is pulling her into the main room.

KATE. What? No!

They are now in the wedding. There are gasps and then everyone falls silent as STEVE *grabs a microphone.*

STEVE. Before you say anything, I want to apologise. This is going to be messy. I didn't want messy. But the thing is I mapped everything out, I thought everything through, and I was thinking so much, I stopped feeling. Carina, you and me are only right on paper. We're wrong everywhere else. And Kate, you open my heart. I thought I wanted a map and really I want someone to get lost with. Let's go.

But suddenly CARINA *is there.*

From this point on, there are no costume changes; changes of role are indicated simply by the actors. It should be a bit jumbled and farcical.

CARINA. No fucking way!

STEVE. Carina –

CARINA. Don't let her bewitch you, Steve! Look at me. Look in my eyes.

STEVE. That isn't going to work.

CARINA. She's completely wrong for you. Walk out that door and you'll be miserable. You'll regret it for the rest of your life.

STEVE. I might.

CARINA. So don't do it, Steve.

STEVE. I have to.

CARINA. But you can't. I love you!

STEVE. I'm sorry.

CARINA. All you ever do is apologise!

JOE *is there too.*

JOE. *That* was a speech! That was something to tell your grandchildren!

KATE. I told you to wait in the car, Dad.

JOE. And miss that speech? He was fantastic! And you! That took guts, what you just did. I'm so happy for you, darling. I'm so happy I can't speak.

KATE. Dad?

JOE. I thought I ruined everything for you. It was killing me!

KATE. You weren't ever going to call Morag, were you?

JOE. No.

KATE. You lied to me!

JOE (*shrugs*). It was for a good cause. (*Beat.*) Now go and be with your husband. And don't make the mistake I made. Hold on to him. Don't ever let him go. And give me back my keys. You want to drive like James Bond, get your own car.

KATE (*gives him back the keys*). I love you, Dad.

ROSS *butts in.*

ROSS. You've got to write this up now.

KATE. Fuck off, Ross.

ROSS. I'm not taking no for an answer. This is *gold.*

And now MORAG *is there.*

MORAG. You can't do this. I didn't bring you up to be stupid, I didn't bring you up to be selfish. I will not sit back and watch you ruin your life.

STEVE. But I don't love her, Mum!

MORAG. She's perfect for you.

STEVE. I don't want perfect. I want to mess up my life my own way. Just like you did.

MORAG. Don't turn this back on me. This is your life, your fuck-up, and don't think I'm going to apologise because I won't.

STEVE. You never do! You always do what you want and now I want to do what I want too. I love her, Mum. I love her like mad.

MORAG (*smiles*). Oh fuck it, there's no saving you.

STEVE (*smiles*). Nope.

MORAG. That's the best I can do about a blessing. Go on if you're going. Go.

ROSS *is back.*

ROSS. Jenny! Get in here! You have to see this. *Jenny!*

KATE *and* STEVE *just look at each other. Then they run.*

Scene Five

A couple of streets away. They run on, out of breath and laughing. He stops. He has hiccups.

STEVE. I never get hiccups.

KATE. It's okay, I've got a great new way of stopping hiccups.

STEVE. Not vodka…

KATE (*laughs*). No, just breathe with me. (*Puts her hand on his arm.*) Get in sync. Nice deep breaths, in and out. It's all about breathing. The rhythm breaks, you have to get it back on track. Just breathe.

They breathe together.

There you go. See?

And then she hiccups. He laughs.

STEVE. Now what?

KATE. I know.

STEVE. What?

KATE. Another way to change the rhythm.

They kiss. When they separate they are both cured. Big romantic finish.

The End.